Mike & ...

MAD ABOUT MARRIAGE

Pacific Press® Publishing Association
Nampa, Idaho
Oshawa, Ontario, Canada
www.pacificpress.com

Cover design by Steve Lanto
Cover image of authors provided by the authors
Inside design by Aaron Troia

The author assumes full responsibility for the accuracy of all facts
and quotations as cited in this book.

Scripture quotations marked ESV are from The Holy Bible, English
Standard Version® (ESV®), copyright © 2001 by Crossway, a publishing ministry of Good News Publishers. Used by permission. All
rights reserved.

You can obtain additional copies of this book by calling toll-free
1-800-765-6955 or by visiting http://www.adventistbookcenter.com.

Library of Congress Cataloging-in-Publication Data:

Tucker, Mike (Michael Duane)
  Mad about marriage / Mike and Gayle Tucker.
     p. cm.
  ISBN 13: 978-0-8163-2410-1
  ISBN 10: 0-8163-2410-7
  1. Spouses—Religious life. 2. Marriage—Religious aspects—
Seventh-day Adventists. I. Tucker, Gayle. II. Title.
  BV4596.M3T83 2010
  248.8'44088286732—dc22
                                                    2010010650

10 11 12 13 14 • 5 4 3 2 1

Contents

As You Begin . . .

"The marriage state, with or without the affection suitable to it, is the completest image of Heaven and Hell we are capable of receiving in this life."
—*Richard Steele,* The Spectator

This book is written in conjunction with a series of *Lifestyle Magazine* television programs about marriage. The underlying thought is that something is wrecking marriages in America. We planned to identify what is doing that and talk about cures, and we wanted a catchy name for this series of programs.

As we began to brainstorm names, our thoughts turned to the great contrasts between people's experiences with marriage. Some are absolutely thrilled to be married, while others can't think of a worse form of torture. Eventually, we settled on a title that appeared to capture both ends of the marital spectrum: *Mad About Marriage.*

I posted our new title on my Facebook account and asked for reactions. The responses I received told me the title was on target. One of my friends said something to the effect of "Well, since my wife just left me and is filing for divorce tomorrow, you could say I'm mad about marriage. In fact, I'm just plain mad! *Furious* would be a better word, but *mad* will suffice." That same day, I received a response from a woman whose feelings about marriage were quite different. She complimented us: "Great title! I'm one of those who is madly in love with my husband."

Madly in love or just plain mad—which best describes you? Or do you migrate back and forth between the two camps? When my wife, Gayle, and I present seminars on marriage, we often speak of God's plan for it. We speak of genuine intimacy, of "two becoming one." Some of those in attendance tell us that their marriage isn't all that bad, but it isn't all that good either.

They long for more, but life is so busy and so much time has elapsed during which the two of them have settled for the status quo that they're almost afraid to rock the boat. What if they bring up their desire for something better and their partner isn't interested or doesn't have the energy? Wouldn't the rejection be worse than just hanging on to what they have?

Others have experienced so much pain for so long due to an unfaithful partner or an addicted partner or an angry or abusive partner that they aren't interested in saving their marriage. In spite of pressures from friends, family, and even the church to stay together, they want out—*now*!

Often couples attend seminars or study self-help books on marriage in the hope of finding a solution to their failing marriage. They learn skills, practice new "languages," and incorporate new behaviors, but nothing seems to make a difference. What they've failed to understand is that something major is wrong—something that could undo all the good that new skills, languages, or behaviors might otherwise be able to accomplish. As long as this destructive force continues to exist in the marriage, improved skills and romantic getaways will not only fail to help, they may actually make matters worse.

One thing is certain: ignoring the problem won't make it better. If we continue to do the same things we've always done, we'll continue to get the same results we've always gotten. So, perhaps it's time to try something new—something different. Let's be brave enough to talk about whatever it is that's ripping your heart out, whether it's your husband's obsession with pornography or your wife's disdain for sex. Maybe we really should talk about that addiction, those finances, or the abusive words, the hitting, the anger. I truly believe you can have something better than what you now experience. There are answers for your problems—solutions to your dilemmas.

In this book we will address some of the things most responsible for wrecking marriages. It may well be that your previous attempts at a happy marriage have failed because you haven't dealt with one of these issues, and the negative undercurrent it has left has been too much to overcome.

As we face these issues, we'll discover that it really is possible to flip the switch from "just plain mad" to "madly in love"!

Chapter 1
Mad About Pornography

"When a girl marries, she exchanges the attentions of many men for the inattention of one."

—*Helen Rowland*

I have seldom seen so great a contrast in a woman. Before Karen married, she was happy, confident, and flirtatious. She enjoyed life and was involved in innumerable activities at school, church, and civic clubs. Her outlook on life was positive. But just five years after her marriage to Ted, Karen was a different woman. In fact, she was scarcely recognizable.

When we spoke privately, Karen said, "I believe I could dance naked in front of my husband, and he would rather watch dots on his computer screen. I just can't compete with pornography."

Karen isn't alone in her frustration. Pornography is having a pernicious effect on marriages across the globe. And it's no longer limited to magazines or videos. Pornography is a booming business on the Internet. Photographs, videos, chat rooms, and live interactions are all available with just a mouse click. Cybersex is fast becoming the number one addiction in the world.

Just how big is this problem? HealthyMind.com reports that worldwide revenues for the pornography industry top fifty-seven billion dollars annually. More than twelve billion dollars of that revenue comes from the United States and two-and-a-half billion of the U.S. revenue goes to Internet porn. To place this in perspective, twelve billion dollars is more than the combined annual revenues of all professional football, baseball, and basketball franchises. And you thought Americans were addicted to sports!

The National Coalition for the Protection of Children and Families estimates that forty million people in the United States are engaged in some sort of sexualized activity on the Internet. They further state that "sex" is the number one topic searched on the Internet, with one-quarter of all searches being related to porn. Eight percent of all e-mails are porn related, and 12 percent of all Web sites are pornographic. Are you as stunned by this as I am?

In a 2003 poll, 47 percent of families said pornography is a problem in their home, while 20 percent of men and 13 percent of women acknowledged that they looked at pornography while at work. And in one study, 10 percent of adults *admitted* to having an addiction to Internet porn.[1] It makes you wonder how many more are addicted but refuse to admit it.

Sexual addictions are progressive by nature. By that I mean that while people may begin with soft porn, eventually that no longer satisfies, and they must move on to more stimulating material. Eventually, people who began with soft porn photos will find themselves using hardcore pornographic material in order to get the same buzz they formerly got from soft porn. Massive exposure to pornography encourages a desire for increasingly deviant materials that involve violence, sadomasochism, and rape.

So it's clear that pornography is widespread, lucrative, and addictive. But does it really affect a person's marriage?

The answer is a resounding Yes! Here's the evidence. Divorce attorneys report that pornography is a factor in two out of three divorces. And researchers have shown that pornography leads men and women to experience conflict and sexual dissatisfaction. In fact, one study conducted by Indiana University concluded that just six hours of exposure to soft-core porn is enough to destroy the viewer's satisfaction with his or her spouse.

Destructive to marriage

Why is pornography so destructive to marriage? Let's begin with the fact that anyone or anything that robs people of their spouse's time and personal and sexual attention will be harmful to their marriage. Without a doubt, involvement with pornography fits into that category. It leaches time and attention from a person's spouse. In fact, it wouldn't be out of line to say that the use of pornography affects a marriage much the same as does an affair.

Marriage is a contract of exclusivity. When people meet certain needs through some other means than the marriage relationship, they've violated their marriage. One of those needs is that of sexual satisfaction. Pornography attempts to satisfy the need for sexual satisfaction outside the bonds of marriage. This robs the spouse of the sexual attention that should have been reserved solely for them.

Pornography devalues and objectifies people. Women in particular feel devalued by pornography. They tend to feel that they aren't good enough, pretty enough, or satisfying enough for their spouse. When a man uses pornography, he sends the message to his wife that, as a woman, she simply doesn't measure up.

As it is, even aside from pornography, Western culture tends to make women feel inferior. Every woman they see on television is thin, beautiful, and sexy. The women who appear in magazines and on the Internet also seem perfect in every way. However, the truth is that many have cosmetic surgery, pay a personal trainer, and starve themselves in order to look that way. On top of that, most of the photographs are manipulated to make these actresses and models look even better. This creates a totally unrealistic idea of womanhood—an unhealthy picture of what it means to be a woman. Yet women are regularly subjected to it, and they feel they can't compete.

Pornographers are selling fantasy, and the fantasy is a lie! That twenty-two-year-old girl in the video isn't interested in the typical porn addict. She's interested in the money fools will pay for her videos, photos, or chat-room time!

A wedge

Pornography drives a wedge between husbands and wives. In her book *An Affair of the Mind,* Laurie Hall put it this way:

Although I was careful with my clothes and figure, I

found that my husband was increasingly critical of the way I looked. Even when friends and acquaintances told me I was an attractive woman, I wasn't attractive enough to compete with eternally young, surgically altered models. [My husband] also expressed dissatisfaction when I was uncomfortable participating in some of the practices he had seen on the Internet. He lost interest in me as a partner. It created such despair in me that I began to let my appearance go. At last, I looked the way his rejection made me feel—totally unlovely.[2]

When the one man whose acceptance was vital to Laurie's emotional well-being rejected her, she felt inadequate, ugly, and undesirable. Her experience strikes a respondent chord with most women whose husbands are involved with pornography. Is it any wonder that pornography is destroying marriages today?

While we could write more about the nature and severity of the problem, let's turn now to solutions. If your spouse is using pornography, it's important that you share your concern about how it is affecting your marriage. Speak of its effect on you and your self-worth, of the feelings of inadequacy and the sense of rejection it gives you. Share how you believe this problem is affecting your sex life and your relationship with your spouse.

Urge your spouse to seek help with the problem. Rather than condemning, share your willingness to do whatever you can to assist as together you break down this obstacle to intimacy. Offer to help find resources for dealing with the problem, and be ready to stand by your spouse during the tough process of breaking the addiction.

If your spouse refuses to address the problem when you have shared your concerns, it may be appropriate for you to draw some boundaries. Proper boundaries are expressions of your respect for yourself, your spouse, and the mutual commitments you have made. They are essential for healthy relationships and can serve as a protection for you and your family.

When establishing boundaries, never make idle threats. Don't draw lines that you aren't willing to defend. For instance, don't threaten to leave your spouse if he or she continues to use pornography unless you are prepared to actually do it.

If you are the partner who is using pornography, the first step to healing your marriage is to admit that you have a problem. This is not an easy step to take. You'll likely find it very difficult to admit that pornography has a grip on you and that you may not be able to handle the problem alone. However, you'll never find freedom from pornography and its devastating effects on your life and your marriage until you admit that you have a problem.

Once you admit to the problem, it is important to look for help. You may need to seek professional counseling or to join a group such as Sexaholics Anonymous.

For most people, accountability is key to recovery. You probably shouldn't have your spouse be the person who holds you accountable. Instead, that person should be a same-gender, third party with whom you will be completely honest. Sexual-addiction groups can help you find this kind of person.

Recovery from the pernicious effects of pornography happens one day at a time. Don't think about how long your recovery may take or how long it has taken. Deal only with today. The addiction didn't develop in one day, and it won't be broken in one day.

By freeing your life of pornography, you will change your attitudes toward your spouse and children, feel better about yourself, have fewer bouts with depression, provide a better role-model for your children, and improve your satisfaction with your marriage and sex life. There is no down side to ending your use of pornography.

---

1. Jerry Ropelato, "Top 10 Internet Pornography Statstics," TopTen Reviews, http://www.internetfilterreview.com/internet-pornography-statistics.html (accessed September 2003).

2. Laurie Hall, *An Affair of the Mind* (n.p.: Focus on the Family, 1998).

Chapter 2
Mad About Infidelity

As I write this chapter, the news outlets are filled with reports that one of the most recognizable sports stars in the world has just admitted to an extramarital affair that lasted nearly three years, and almost daily there are new reports of his sexual dalliances with a wide variety of women. Whether any of these reports are true is anyone's guess. There appears to be a bit of a feeding frenzy as every news organization is sleuthing around in an attempt to find dirt on this man's previously squeaky clean reputation. I have no desire to trash this man, so I won't mention his name here. Instead, I'm praying for him, his family, and his marriage.

Few things have as devastating an effect on the viability of a marriage as infidelity. Nothing tears at the fabric of a relationship quite like the jolt of learning that one's spouse has broken the promise of "forsaking all others." The pain of that rejection is a difficult thing to get over.

Melanie and Brad had been married for nearly fifteen years. Brad was an entrepreneur who was totally dedicated to the success of his businesses. Although he made a tremendous amount of money, he worked long hours and lived with a lot of stress, and his hard-nosed business persona was difficult to turn off when he was home. He tended to give orders to his wife and children, causing Melanie to feel more like his employee than his wife.

When Brad and Melanie's children started school, Melanie had a lot of spare time on her hands. Since she wasn't limited by a lack of money, she busied herself by redecorating their home.

Bill, one of the subcontractors Melanie worked with, was young, extremely handsome, and obviously interested in Melanie. He listened to her ideas, praised her for her excellent taste, and told her she had a real eye for decorating. Melanie found herself looking forward to her time with this man. He was meeting needs that Brad didn't seem to know she had. Before long, Melanie and Bill were involved in a torrid affair.

When Brad first learned of Melanie's infidelity, he wanted to get vengeance on her and her lover. But eventually, Brad got past the anger and told Melanie that he wanted to forgive her and to save their marriage. He knew the work would be incredibly hard, but he was willing to do whatever it took, including selling the business if necessary. He would go to counseling and find new ways of relating to her if she would end the affair.

Melanie was surprised by Brad's reaction. His willingness to forgive her was extremely attractive, and at first, she was determined to forsake her lover and make the marriage work. But though she tried, she couldn't quit seeing Bill. She kept going back to him in spite of Brad's pleading. Eventually, Melanie chose her lover over Brad and her children, and the marriage ended in divorce.

Can a marriage survive an affair? Should people even try to save a marriage once infidelity has occurred?

Infidelity or adultery is usually defined as voluntary sexual intercourse between a married person and someone other than his or her spouse. However, experts aren't certain that this definition is broad enough. There is a growing consensus that infidelity is not limited to sexual unfaithfulness, but that it also occurs when a spouse forms a strong emotional attachment outside of marriage.

The term *affair* can cover intense but nonsexual relationships, purely sexual relationships in which there is no emotional bond, or both sexual and emotional involvement. Essentially, any secret sexual or romantic relationship outside of one's marriage constitutes infidelity.

How common are extramarital affairs? No one knows for sure. Studies conducted over the past twelve years estimate that anywhere from 22 to 68 percent of men and 14 to 66 percent of women have engaged in infidelity or adultery. That's a huge spread, but it's difficult to establish firm statistics on something that is by nature very secretive. However, in a recent conversation I had with psychologist and author Dr. Willard Harley, he said that approximately 50 percent of all marriages will be affected by an affair. I tend to believe that his estimates are close to the truth.

Devastating effects

While experts may debate exactly how many people cheat on their spouse, what is *not* debated is the long-lasting and devastating effects that infidelity has on the marriage relationship, the offended partner, the children, and even the unfaithful partner. An affair is by nature a lie. It is a lie to one's spouse, but it is also a lie that is believed by those who are involved in the affair. Here's how it works. The possibility of being discovered multiplies the emotional intensity of the affair. This creates an adrenaline rush that is so strong that it makes the parties involved in the affair feel that they've never experienced such deep love and such exciting sex. They think that anything this intense, this great, must be strong enough to last forever. This is the real thing—right?

Wrong! Those who divorce as a result of an affair seldom marry the person with whom they are having the affair. Dr. Jan Halper's study of successful men found that very few men who have affairs divorce their wives and marry their lovers—only 3 percent of the 4,100 successful men surveyed did so.[1]

Frank Pittman has found that the divorce rate among those who did marry their lovers was 75 percent. The reasons for the high divorce rate include guilt, unmet expectations, the eventual intervention of reality, and a distrust of both marriage and the other party in the affair.[2]

Why is infidelity so destructive? An affair breaks trust. If people can't trust their mate on this most basic commitment, how can they believe anything else the mate says? Why would they entrust their emotions or their future well-being to someone who has demonstrated that he or she is unworthy of their trust?

Infidelity also has a tremendous effect on self-esteem. It leaves the offended party asking questions such as, "Why would she need someone else? Am I not handsome enough, thin enough, wealthy enough, smart enough, educated enough, or . . . ?"

The unfaithful partner experiences a blow to his or her self-esteem as well. Most will at some point ask themselves something such as, "What kind of person am I? Why would I do such a terrible thing to my spouse and my children?"

In most cases, children shouldn't be told of a parent's infidelity. Knowing about it does nothing of value for them. Often, children view a parent's infidelity as a personal betrayal. Later, in adulthood, they may wonder if they have inherited the tendency to be unfaithful to a partner. Fear of commitment and a distrust of self can plague them as adults.

When the affair results in a divorce, the effects on the children are multiplied. A divorce signals the collapse of the family structure. The very foundation of the children's life crumbles, and their whole world is shaken. Children feel alone and very frightened.

In his book *Children and Divorce: What to Expect, How to Help,* Dr. Archibald Hart says that in part, divorce brings suffering to children because after the divorce, parents have a diminished capacity to parent. During the critical months or even years of the divorce, they are preoccupied with their own survival. Dr. Hart further states that the divorce creates conflicts between the children's loyalties. Whose side do they take? Often children feel pulled in both directions.[3]

Mad About Infidelity

The children of divorce face other issues too. There's the fear caused by the anger and resentment that their parents express. And there's the deep-seated insecurity caused by uncertainty about the future, the family's diminished financial status, and—if they are moved—the loss of the familiar church, school, and friends, which can result in deep depression.

Countless studies demonstrate that children of divorce are more susceptible to disease, experience more psychosomatic illness, score lower in school, have more interpersonal conflict and therefore tend to get into more trouble at school, are more likely to question their sexual identity, are more likely to act out sexually, are much more likely to suffer from frequent episodes of depression, and are at 50 percent greater risk for divorce when they marry. Truancy and juvenile delinquency are much higher in children of divorce. And it's much more difficult for them to form healthy emotional attachments.

The bottom line is that the myth of resilience can be quite destructive since it can leave children at great risk. Make no mistake about it, divorce has devastating effects on children—effects that may last an entire lifetime. So, those who decide to try to save their marriage after their partner's infidelity may be giving their children a gift of inestimable value. And since a divorce could easily cause parents to miss a great deal of the lives of their children, fighting for their marriage can be a great gift to themselves as well.

It has been said that you should never stay married for the sake of the children. I couldn't disagree more strongly. Making a choice for the benefit of your children is rarely the wrong thing to do. Cases of abuse and serial adultery are exceptions to this rule, but other than that, there are few things that would make the decision to divorce the right decision for your children and therefore the right decision for you. Your happiness or unhappiness is not reason enough to place your children at risk. A better choice is for husbands and wives to decide to do the incredibly hard work necessary to save the marriage, if for no other reason than for the well-being of their children.

Recovery

How can people save their marriage when an affair has occurred?

The survival of a marriage in the aftermath of an affair depends upon whether the cheater can see and acknowledge the pain he or she has caused the spouse. The one who had the affair must do this without defending his or her actions. Offering a "reason" for the affair is little more than a thinly veiled rationalization of the infidelity. Acknowledging the pain the affair has caused without defending the affair displays the vulnerability and remorse that make healing a possibility.

Often it is much harder for the "innocent" spouses to recover. Their recovery will be greatly facilitated if they are given an appropriate time and place in which to express the pain they feel. Then healing can begin.

Recovery requires the "guilty" party to break off all contact with the illegitimate lover. Any contact will thwart the recovery process and place the marriage at tremendous risk.

Affairs rarely happen in marriages that don't already have some dysfunction. Eventually, it will be necessary for the "innocent party" to acknowledge aloud that his or her own behavior has contributed to the "guilty" party's feeling that he or she had to go outside the marriage to satisfy unmet needs. This acknowledgement, accompanied by appropriate behavioral and attitude changes, will provide an opportunity to heal the relationship.

Ultimately, a work of forgiveness must be done. Forgiving someone is never an easy thing to do, but no marriage can survive without it. For help with this process, read the chapter on forgiveness in this book.

If you have already experienced the nightmare of infidelity,

Mad About Infidelity

I offer this word of hope: not only can you survive this nightmare, you can actually emerge from it with a stronger and more fulfilling marriage than you have ever dreamed possible.

I remember when Tom and Casey came to me for counseling. Actually, Tom had to drag Casey into my office. She was one of the angriest women I'd ever met. She was mad about her husband's infidelity. She didn't just want out of the marriage, she wanted her husband to suffer! She'd been betrayed, and she wanted vengeance.

I doubt that Casey would have agreed to go to counseling at all had it not been for their three daughters. They loved their daddy and didn't know anything about his indiscretion. Casey knew that a divorce would radically alter their lives, so, reluctantly, she accompanied Tom to my office. It took a lot of work for Casey to forgive her husband, but eventually she did. Then the two of them worked to rebuild trust and to strengthen their marriage.

Recently, I received an e-mail from Casey. In it, she reminded me of our first meeting. At that meeting, I told her that not only could her marriage survive this blow, but it could actually become stronger than it had been before. Casey wrote that she didn't believe me then, but now she knows that I was right. She claims that she has never felt closer to Tom than she does today. She said, "I am so thankful that I forgave Tom and chose to stay with him."

Casey said that every day, little things make her aware of just how good her life is now. When she sees one of her daughters sitting in her daddy's lap or watches as Tom plays catch with the girls or hears them tell him about their day at school, she is reminded that none of this would have happened had she not chosen to forgive her husband's infidelity.

Casey told me about something that had happened the previous Christmas. The family was decorating the Christmas tree one evening, and after nearly all the decorations were in place, as

Tom lifted one of their daughters up to put the angel on the top of the Christmas tree, he looked over at Casey and with tears in his eyes he just mouthed the words "Thank you!" Nothing else, just "Thank you!" Casey said, "I knew that he was thankful for that moment—to be there to see it. And I was thankful too that God saw us through so we can experience all these gifts together. So now I know that the 'little' things in life are really the 'big' things."

While Casey would have never chosen the pain Tom's infidelity brought her, she has learned that it is possible to grow through such an experience. Casey and Tom found help for this process in their faith. She said, "I am thankful that even in a big mess, our wonderful Lord can bring out a beautiful thing."

Casey and Tom's experience reminds us that there is hope for marriages torn apart by infidelity. Your marriage can survive and even thrive. Don't lose hope.

---

1. Jan Halper, *Quiet Desperation: The Truth About Successful Men* (New York: WarnerBooks, 1988).

2. Frank Pittman, *Private Lies: Infidelity and the Betrayal of Intimacy* (New York: Norton, 1989).

3. Archibald Hart, *Children and Divorce: What to Expect, How to Help* (Dallas: Word Publishing, 1996).

Chapter 3
Mad About Addiction

Bill was a professional with work that was satisfying and paid well. And Bill was fortunate enough to have two wonderful sons who were the joy of his life.

But an accident left Bill with a lot of pain. He started to self-medicate and he was doing anything he had to do to get the prescription meds. And whenever that failed, he turned to alcohol.

Of course, the addiction affected Bill's performance at work, but the main problem for Carmela, his wife, was Bill's relationship with her and their boys. Bill absented himself from family activities, falsely blaming work responsibilities.

As Carmela described the situation to me, it was obvious that her family was going through all the usual stages that families of addicts experience: First, Bill and Carmela went into denial. They tried to explain away what was happening. Then they tried to eliminate the problem. Carmela pressured Bill to quit, all the while covering for him in order to keep up a good front. Finally, chaos and disorganization took over. Carmela couldn't pretend anymore. Bill became more withdrawn and angry. And the boys knew things weren't right and began to act out. That's when Carmela felt she had to get help and came to me.

I wish I could tell you that the end of the story was positive. Unfortunately, Bill's addictions finally claimed his marriage, as they so often do. Marriage vows call implicitly for total honesty, but addiction is built upon secrets and lies. That causes a rip in the fabric of relationships, placing marriages at great risk.

When a husband or wife is actively drinking or drugging, the entire family suffers. Children may become caretakers of the addicted parent. The nonaddicted spouse of an alcoholic or addicted partner may become stressed or depressed and almost certainly becomes codependent. Family members become anxious and hypervigilant because the addicted mate or parent often experiences extreme mood swings. The family members find themselves walking on eggshells as they await the next drunken or drugged episode, which is certain to wreak havoc on the home and marriage.

For families of addicts, home is no longer a sanctuary. It becomes an unsafe place where rage often erupts into violence. Friends dwindle as the family isolates themselves in order to maintain "appearances." Feelings of anger, frustration, and hopelessness are buried but tend to resurrect themselves in a myriad of physical, emotional, and mental illnesses. The nonaddicted spouse may question his or her own sanity amid all the deceit, abusive behavior, and crumbling dreams.

There is a powerful link between alcoholism and divorce. Alison Clarke-Stewart and Cornelia Brentano are authors of the book *Divorce: Causes and Consequences.*[1] They cite numerous studies that confirm that "people who drink more are more likely to divorce." The authors note that people who are divorced consume the highest levels of alcohol, and, conversely, people who are married have the lowest levels of alcohol consumption. They add that while alcoholics are just as likely to get married as nonalcoholics, their divorce or separation rate is at least four times that of the general population.

A 2007 study by researchers at the nonprofit Rand Corporation looked at divorce rates among young adults. The researchers found that the primary cause of divorces that occurred by age twenty-nine is heavy drinking by one or the other of the marriage partners.[2]

While alcoholism and divorce certainly go hand-in-hand, ending the marriage is not necessarily the only option. If the addict is truly willing to seek help, it is possible to deal effectively with the problem. However, if the alcoholic refuses to seek help and is creating a home environment where abuse takes place or has the potential to occur, it is important for the alcoholic's partner and children to get out as soon as possible.

It should be noted that family members who live with an addict have been damaged by the experience and will need support during the process of familial reconciliation. Organizations such as Al-Anon and Alateen have been providing help to family members of alcoholics for more than fifty years.

Gender differences

Jean Kinney says that women who are married to alcoholics and have children at age eighteen and under will almost always stay in the marriage. In fact, 90 percent of women make that choice, whereas 90 percent of men in the same situation will leave. Women seem to be less willing to trust their own judgment. They tend to defer to their husband and thereby defer to the addiction.[3]

Husbands who are addicted are either unwilling or unable to meet the intimacy needs of their wives. As a result, women in marriages with addicts have much lower self-esteem. And on the whole, wives feel overly responsible for the success of the marriage. They either blame themselves for their husband's addiction or they blame themselves for "picking the wrong person."

In fact, a woman who is in love with an alcoholic becomes an addict herself. Her husband infects her with the addiction. That's why, unless someone helps her, she will marry the same type of man over and over again.

But it is not just the wife who is negatively affected by a man's addiction. Daughters of alcoholics and other addicts are negatively affected as well. Not only do they suffer from low self-esteem, but they also score the highest on self-condemnation scales.

Most men respond to an alcoholic or addicted spouse differently than women do. Men tend to be either unable or unwilling to express their emotions. It's not that they don't feel anything—they do feel deeply. But they don't know what to do with their emotions, so they tend to stuff them or ignore them.

Intimacy becomes an issue as well. Many men find nonsexual intimacy with a woman to be challenging in the best of circumstances. But men who are married to alcoholics doubt that they can establish intimacy in any way other than sexually. Yet they find it almost impossible to trust that their addicted wife can be sexually faithful.

Marriage with an alcoholic or addict isn't really a marriage. The addict will always choose the drug over the marriage, and anyone who has a commitment that supersedes their commitment to their spouse and family (other than to God) is unfaithful to the marriage vows.

If you are married to an addicted or alcoholic spouse, you must get help. If you are the one who has the addiction, you need to enter detoxification and treatment before undergoing therapy for your addiction. Your marriage won't survive unless both of you get help.

I don't believe in divorce. I firmly believe that people should stay in their marriage until it becomes impossible to remain there. But if it's impossible to be sober together, or if continued substance abuse and addiction have created an environment that is too toxic for the family to be emotionally, physically, and spiritually safe and healthy, divorce may be an option. However, people shouldn't choose this "nuclear option" until they've exhausted every other one. They should fight for their marriage until it becomes obvious that there is no longer a marriage to fight for.

The Community Alcohol Information Program in New Hampshire suggests that there are six stages in a marriage with an alcoholic/addict.[4]

1. Denial. During this stage, both partners attempt to explain away occasional episodes of excessive drinking or drug abuse.

2. Attempts to eliminate the problem. In this stage, the nonaddicted spouse realizes that the drinking or drug use isn't normal and attempts to pressure their spouse either to quit, to cut down, or to be more careful. During this stage, in an effort to maintain a good front, the nonaddicted spouse will attempt to hide the problem from those outside the home.

3. Disorganization and chaos. Eventually, efforts to hide the problem become ineffective as the using spouse finds it impossible to quit or cut down. Life tends to be a series of crises. It is now impossible to pretend that everything is OK. This is when the spouse is likely to seek outside help.

4. Reorganization in spite of the problem. In this stage, the non-using spouse's coping abilities have become strengthened. He or she gradually assumes a larger share of the responsibility for the family and depends less and less on the substance-abusing spouse.

5. Efforts to escape. The nonusing spouse may attempt a separation or divorce. If the family remains intact, the family members will continue to live around the alcoholic. They learn to depend less on the substance-abusing spouse as they attempt to minimize that person's destructive influence on the family.

6. Family reorganization. If a divorce or separation occurs, the family will reorganize without the alcoholic family member. If the alcoholic/addict achieves sobriety, reconciliation may be possible.

Marriages in which substance abuse takes place can be saved if both spouses agree to get help. Healing won't come easily, but with professional help and good outside support, eventually the marriage can survive and even thrive—so don't lose hope!

---

1. Alison Clarke-Stewart and Cornelia Brentano, *Divorce: Causes and Consequences* (Hartford, Conn.: Yale University Press, 2006).

2. Rebecca L. Collins, Phyllis L. Ellickson, and David J. Klein, "The Role of Substance Use in Young Adult Divorce," *Addiction* 102, no. 5 (May 2007): 786–794.

3. Jean Kinney, *Loosening the Grip: A Handbook of Alcohol Information,* 6th ed. (New York: McGraw-Hill, 2000).

4. As cited in an article by Erica Orloff, "Can Marriage Survive Addiction?" Full Spectrum Recovery, http://www.fullspectrumrecovery.com/control/articles/uploaded/Can%20Marriage%20Survive%20Addict.pdf.

Chapter 4
Mad About Abuse

In this book we are dealing with the really big issues that are destroying marriages today. None is bigger than that of abuse.

Barbara Hart, a national expert on family violence, defines domestic violence this way: "Domestic violence involves a continuum of behaviors ranging from degrading remarks to cruel jokes, economic exploitation, punches and kicks, false imprisonment, sexual abuse, suffocating actions, maiming assaults, and homicide. Unchecked, domestic violence usually increases in frequency and severity. Many victims suffer all forms of abuse. Verbal and emotional abuse may be subtler than physical harm, but this does not mean that it is less destructive to victims. Many have said that the emotional scars take much longer to heal than the broken bones."[1]

Let's establish one important truth before we continue: abuse is *never* the fault of the victim. No one can force another person to become abusive. Abuse— whether it's physical, emotional, verbal, sexual, or spiritual abuse—is always the fault of and the responsibility of the abuser and not the victim.

As surely as I have written this, some who read these words will respond with something to the effect of "I'm sure that is true for most people, but in my case—" If you are the victim of abuse and find yourself thinking similar thoughts, you are engaging in "victim think." You have been trained to think like a victim, and as long as you continue to think like a victim, you will be vulnerable to abuse.

Spousal abuse is a growing and extremely dangerous problem. Here are the ugly facts: One in four women will know domestic violence in her lifetime. Domestic violence is the leading predictor of child abuse. Boys who witness domestic violence in their homes are fifteen hundred times more likely to perpetrate abuse later in life. And 50 percent of girls growing up in an abusive home will go on to be victims of abuse themselves.

Abuse follows predictable patterns. And unless the cycle is broken, it also tends to escalate in intensity and frequency.

Often, the abuse begins with attempts to isolate the victim. The abusive husband* will control what his wife does, whom she sees and talks to, what she reads, and where she goes. Abusers limit outside contacts for their victims and will use jealousy to justify their actions.

It isn't uncommon for an abuser to make light of the abuse by refusing to take seriously his victim's concerns about it. He may deny that it actually happened or attempt to shift the responsibility for the abusive behavior to the victim, claiming that she caused it.

If there are children in the marriage, the abuser will use them to make the victim feel guilty. Often, abusers use their children to relay messages to the victim. And abusers may seek to control their victims by threatening to take their children away from them.

Since abusers are usually very insecure people who are seeking power and control, they attempt to use male privilege as a rationale for their behavior. This involves treating their victim like a servant while the abuser acts like the king of the castle. He insists on making all the big decisions, leaving little or nothing for her to decide. He is also determined to be the one who defines gender roles in the relationship.

---

*While either partner in a marriage can abuse, wives are the victims in the majority of cases. So, in this chapter, I have used masculine pronouns when referring to the abuser and feminine pronouns for the victim. However, the descriptions and principles apply to abusers of both sexes.

Economic abuse is another method of gaining control and power. The abuser may prevent his spouse from getting or keeping a job. If he is unemployed or underemployed and her income is greater than his, feelings of impotence will often heighten the abusive behavior. He will make his wife ask for money while withholding information about finances and access to credit and cash. If she has a job and earns her own money, he demands that it be given to him and that he have the power to decide about whether or not she have an allowance and how much it will be.

Abusers may use intimidation—intimidating looks, gestures, and actions—as a means of gaining power and control over the victim. The abuser may destroy the victim's property, abuse her pets, or display weapons in a threatening manner.

Emotional abuse is often just as devastating as physical abuse. In fact, many people think that it is actually worse. Emotional abuse may include put-downs and name-calling. The abuser attempts to make the victim feel bad about herself— about her looks, intelligence, or character. The abuser may play mind games in an attempt to make the victim think she is crazy. Often, he will humiliate her or cause her to feel guilty.

An abuser isn't afraid to use coercion and threats. He may make his spouse participate in humiliating sexual acts, stating that it will make him love her more. Then, when she has complied, he will blackmail her, threatening to tell what she's done if she ever attempts to leave him or if she refuses to comply with his wishes. He may even make his victim perform illegal acts so he can hold them over her head.

When the police have been called because of violent episodes, abusers frequently force their victims to drop charges. They often accomplish this by threatening to hurt the victim or by actually hurting her. He may threaten to report the victim to child protective services as an unfit or abusive mother. Or the abuser may pressure his victim by threatening to commit suicide. All of these behaviors are abusive and are therefore incredibly destructive of the marriage.

The cycle of violence

Eventually, violence enters many abusive relationships. Violent abuse follows a very predictable pattern. Typically, a confrontation results in violence, for which the abuser becomes apologetic and self-effacing. He makes promises, and, for a while, he makes good on those promises, often becoming extremely kind, thoughtful, and caring. The battering stops, and the victim believes that things are getting better.

But as time passes, the attentive behavior decreases and the abuser becomes irritated over small issues. Tension begins to build, but it seems manageable enough.

Then, the tension escalates. The abuser's irritation increases, and he may erupt in verbal or emotional abuse.

Finally, the increasing tension explodes in another violent episode, usually worse than the previous one. And then the cycle starts all over again.

The abuser may run through this pattern in a matter of days or months or even years. Generally, as the couple repeats the cycle, it increases in frequency and/or intensity—the violence becoming more pronounced and more dangerous.

This pattern will not correct itself. Nor can the victim prevent it, even though the abuser has caused her to believe that she is to blame. Left unchecked, this pattern may even result in the death of the victim.

Well-intentioned religious leaders often encourage a wife who is being victimized by an abusive spouse to remain with the spouse and submit to him. These religious leaders could actually be signing the victim's death warrant if there is no intervention! This is not an overstatement of the facts.

Attempts to stop the abuse through marriage counseling, anger-management courses, or even psychotherapy are rarely helpful. In fact, these things often make the problem worse. One of the reasons that traditional marriage counseling fails to help cases of spousal abuse is that this type of counseling assumes that the partners are equals. This is not the case in abusive relationships.

If you are experiencing domestic abuse, here is what you need to know: the abuse and violence are *not* your fault. You are a victim, and victims are never the cause of abuse. While you aren't a perfect person, nothing you have done causes, warrants, or excuses violent or demeaning behavior from your spouse. This is a behavior he chooses and for which he bears responsibility.

Know that you are not alone. The police and the courts can help you because abuse is a crime. Also, most communities have domestic violence programs with caring people who are trained to help you.

It is important for you to develop a safety plan. Keep money, important documents, a change of clothes, and an extra set of keys in a safe place, such as with a friend or neighbor. And talk to a trusted friend, family member, or professional who can help you in a time of need or when you decide you must leave.

If you choose to leave your spouse, it is important that you refuse to go back to the marriage until he has received professional help. While the abuser may apologize and be remorseful, that's not enough. Abuse doesn't stop because the abuser feels bad about what he has done. It stops because a genuine change has been brought about through professional intervention. Abusers need to seek long-term professional help. You shouldn't return until this help is secured and the abuser demonstrates over a lengthy period that he's made a lasting change.

If you've decided to remain in the marriage, keep a log or diary of the abuse. This log should include evidence of threats in letters, e-mails, voicemail, or answering-machine messages. Make a list of the resources available that can help you take care of yourself. This includes emotional support.

Tell a doctor or a nurse about the violence. These professionals can document the abuse in your medical records and take photographs of your injuries that will be helpful should you decide to take legal action. If you are being stalked, contact a shelter or program for abused women and ask for their assistance in obtaining a protective order. Stalking is against the law.

If you have children, you need to develop a safety plan for them too. If you don't know how to do this, contact a shelter for women and ask for help. The National Domestic Violence Hotline is 1-800-799-SAFE (1-800-799-7233).

You are not without resources. You don't have to feel trapped and helpless. Assistance is available. The law is on your side. Seek help now.

A final word: If you were victimized by abuse as a child, whether that abuse was emotional, verbal, physical, or sexual, you owe it to yourself to seek help in recovering from it. Like it or not, you carry that abuse with you in your current relationships. You will never know how good life and love can be until you have addressed the trauma of your childhood and found healing. Competent Christian counselors can help you face your nightmare. Don't allow abuse—whether current or from your childhood—to destroy you or your marriage.

---

1. Barbara J. Hart, *Domestic Violence Overview,* in Manual for the 1st Judicial Circuit Family Violence Symposia (1998), section 1.

Chapter 5
Mad About Negative Communication

Research now proves that the way couples communicate with each other makes a big difference in marital success. In fact, the very best predictors of divorce can be found in patterns of communication between couples. Negative patterns of communication, whether intentional or not, come as close to a guarantee of relationship failure as can be found.

A twenty-year study conducted by Scott Stanley, Howard Markman, and others from the University of Denver found that the existence of one or more negative patterns of communication in a marriage was the most accurate predictor of impending divorce. Their study demonstrated that removing one pattern of negative communication can do more to ensure marital longevity than can adding five elements to the marriage.[1]

Communicating genuine tenderness and love for your spouse is essential. Removing negative communication is the first step toward positive communication and marital stability.

Reporting on their research findings, Stanley and Markman noted four distinct patterns of communication that hurt marriages and are present to one degree or another in nearly every failed relationship.[2]

1. Escalation

The pattern of escalation occurs when a disagreement increases in intensity and volume and even in personal attacks until a small argument becomes a major event.

An example of escalation can be seen in an argument between Maria and Craig.

Mad About Negative Communication

MARIA: Honey, you left the dishes in the sink . . . again.

CRAIG: Oh, I was in a hurry.

MARIA: I guess you're always in a hurry.

CRAIG [*smirking*]: Probably am.

MARIA: It's not hard, you know. I just asked you about a hundred times to rinse them and put them on the counter or in the dishwasher. But you have to pile them up in the sink!

CRAIG: I thought putting them in the sink was better than leaving them on the floor, where the kids left them. And heaven forbid that you should pick them up from there. The sink was made to be used, you know.

MARIA: That's just the point—when it's piled full, I can't use it.

CRAIG: So you're thinking of actually *using* the sink? That'd be a refreshing change.

MARIA: I'll tell you what would be refreshing. It would be refreshing if I could believe anything you say. I ask you to do this one thing about the sink, and you say, "Of course, dear," and then you never do it. Might as well talk to a wall.

CRAIG: Oh, give it a rest. Can't you do anything but nag? When I pick up the dishes, you'd think I might get a little credit. But, no—instead, I get this. Nothing I do is ever right for you, is it?

MARIA: You are unbelievable! You pick up one dish, and you want a standing ovation. You're such a jerk!

CRAIG: What? A jerk? Because I don't get sucked into your OCD? "Stack the dishes this way, fold the towels that way." You've got to be kidding.

MARIA: Just stop it. I work all day at my job and all night at home, and you won't lift a lousy finger. I don't need this.

CRAIG: *You* don't need this? *I* don't need this—and I don't know why I put up with it!

MARIA: Well, no one's begging you to stay!

CRAIG: Fine! I hope you and your sink will be happy together. I'm gone!

It's hard to believe that an argument over dishes in the sink could actually end in threats to leave the marriage. Yet this sort of thing does happen in marriages with great regularity. When it does, deep wounds and lasting scars result. And those wounds are so deep that they block loving messages sent later. The destructive undercurrent of negative communication makes it impossible to perceive those loving messages positively. Learning to discuss problems without wounding each other will free you to feel the tenderness in your partner's words.

2. Invalidation

Invalidation is an attack on the person, character, feelings, or values of one's spouse. This attack may be intentional and openly confrontational, or it can be more subtle and unintentional. Let's view a couple of examples of a subtle form of invalidation.

JANA: Honey, I went to Weight Watchers today.
CLIFF: Oh? How did it go?
JANA: I didn't lose anything. I'm so discouraged.
CLIFF: Well, you know [*he shrugs*], you can't always lose.
JANA: But I really thought I would this week. I should have, with all the work I've done.
CLIFF: Oh, I'm sure it will get better.
JANA: No—you don't understand. I counted every point, every morsel that went into my mouth. I exercised. I did everything right, and I didn't lose anything—not an ounce. It just gets to me. It's like I'll *never* be able to lose weight.
CLIFF: Oh, it's OK. I don't think you should worry about it. [*Pause*] You know, I don't even really like skinny women.

While Cliff may have thought he was being helpful, his comments were anything but. In reality, Cliff made Jana feel that her concern about losing weight was silly and unimportant. She perceived that as a direct attack on her as a person. She felt that either Cliff didn't care how she felt or he was tired of being bothered by her concern. This wasn't what Cliff intended to communicate, but the damage was done anyway.

How our partners perceive our words is important. Having good motives isn't enough. If we want to avoid doing harm to the relationship, we must be aware of how our spouse will interpret our message. And because men and women think and talk differently, we have to work at learning to communicate in a way that our spouse understands.

While there are certainly exceptions, women tend to bond through shared feelings and men through shared activity. When my wife shares a problem with me, usually she doesn't want me to provide a solution. Instead, she wants to feel close to me as I respond to her feelings and empathize with her. Once I understand her opinion and feelings, she may ask for my input. It's dangerous to assume that every woman will feel the same way about this issue, but it's quite safe to say that most women will respond as my wife, Gayle, does. Your wife may be an exception. The only safe course is to ask her how she would prefer for you to respond in a similar situation. If you think you know the answer but are mistaken, your spouse will think your response is uncaring.

Women, as well as men, can unintentionally say things that hurt their spouse. Suppose a man chooses a restaurant for a special occasion with his wife and the service happens to be subpar that evening. If the wife criticizes the service, the man is likely to feel that the criticism is directed toward him rather than toward the restaurant. After all, he made the choice. It's unlikely that the wife intended her criticism of the restaurant to be interpreted as a critique of her husband's ability to choose good restaurants. However, many husbands might see it that way. As Gayle says, "It's a male ego thing."

Invalidation can also be quite overt and intentional. Here's an example:

JERRY: Honey, I hate to tell you, but I got a ticket on the way home.

LINDA: Another ticket?

JERRY: Yeah, I really thought I was—

LINDA [*interrupts*]: You got *another* ticket?

JERRY: Well, yes. But I really thought I was obeying the speed limit.

LINDA: I can't believe you got another ticket. I'm so sick of spending money on your tickets. We could practically buy a car with the money we've wasted on fines, and—

JERRY [*interrupts, still sounding repentant*]: I know, I know. And I've been slowing down. But this time I really didn't think I was speeding.

LINDA [*in a parental voice*]: Right. Well, let me tell you something: people who don't speed don't get tickets.

Speaking to a spouse as one might scold a child communicates that the spouse is stupid or irresponsible. It is a very demeaning way to speak to another adult, and it is always destructive.

The correction for invalidation is validation. We must learn to listen with empathy and communicate with respect. It is never appropriate to speak with a scolding "parental" voice to one's spouse.

Invalidation may also come in other forms that we may not readily recognize. Ignoring your spouse is a form of invalidation, as is habitually interrupting or talking over him or her, especially in the company of other people.*

People who want their marriage to succeed learn how to navigate the communication idiosyncrasies of their mate. They learn to communicate in a way that will ensure that

---

*It's worth noting that parents frequently treat children this way—ignoring, interrupting, or not listening to them. This invalidation takes a toll on their self-esteem and deeply affects their future. This is not what we want for our children.

their mate recognizes and receives their genuine concern. However, no one will ever do this perfectly. There will be times when our best intentions are still misunderstood. It is at those times that we need to trust each other.

3. Negative interpretation

Negative interpretation occurs when one party interprets something that was said more negatively than their spouse intended. In one sense, the person who interprets things negatively is attempting to read their mate's mind. It is as though they're thinking, *I know you're saying one thing, but I believe you actually mean something else.* The following conversation is an example of negative interpretation.

LARRY: Hey, babe, we're getting really close to Thanksgiving.

NANCY: I know, and I'm so excited! We get to have everybody at our house. Hooray!

LARRY: Yeah, it's going to be cool. [*Pause*] I've been thinking about all the cooking you'll be doing, and I thought I might help with Thanksgiving dinner.

NANCY: You? Help with cooking?

LARRY: Well, yeah. I know it's a lot of work, and I thought I could make the candied yams this year. That would take some of the load off.

NANCY: Well, that's sweet, but I always just make the yams along with the rest of the meal. It's not that big a deal.

LARRY: No, but if I can help . . .

NANCY [*looks puzzled, but then a light goes on in her mind*]: You don't *like* my candied yams, do you?

Larry [*surprised, backpedaling*]: No, that's not it. Your candied yams are fine!

NANCY: Now that I think about it, you're always trying to get me to change them. "Honey, why don't you try marshmallow topping this year?" or "Try brown sugar and nuts on top this time." It's always some new request.

LARRY: Your yams are just fine . . . I just like variety. I like to try them a lot of different ways.

NANCY: No . . . No . . . That's it! You don't like my candied yams.

LARRY: No, seriously—that's not it! I just thought maybe I could help with the dinner.

NANCY: *Hmm.* Well, that seems strange to me.

LARRY: I like your candied yams. Really!

NANCY: You know, I'd really rather you just admit it.

Larry shrugs and throws his hands up.

What could Larry have done to have brought about a different outcome?

Actually, there was nothing Larry could have done. The only person who can correct negative interpretations is the person who interprets negatively. Instead of negative mind reading (*You may* say *this, but what you really* mean *is . . .*), they must choose to engage in positive mind reading.

Early in our marriage, Gayle and I stumbled onto a principle that has served as an excellent solution for the problem of negative interpretation. Early on, Gayle did something that hurt me. I told her about it, and she apologized. A little later, I mentioned the incident again. She apologized again. Later, I brought it up again, and she apologized yet again.

After about the fourth time around, she said, "You act as though I did this on purpose."

With my background, that seemed possible, so I replied, "Well, yeah."

Gayle looked directly at me and with deep sincerity said, "I want you to know something. I will *never* intentionally hurt you."

This was a brand-new thought to me, and what a good one! Over the years since then, it has become the mantra for our marriage, our basic assumption: *My spouse would never intentionally hurt me.*

Maintaining this assumption may not sound like much of a solution to you, but believe me, it works! Here's how: it frees me to interpret what my wife says and does more positively than I otherwise might. When Gayle says or does something I don't understand, I don't assume that she meant to harm me because I know she would never intentionally harm me. If what she has said or done hurts me, I simply assume that the pain was inadvertent, as Gayle would never purposefully hurt me. So, I can go to her and say, "I know you aren't aware of this, but what you just said hurt me." And Gayle will reply with an apology and then ask me to help her understand how and why her words or behavior hurt me so she can avoid doing it again. This little agreement between the two of us prevents me from attempting to read her mind.

As of this writing, Gayle and I have been married for more than thirty-four years, and I can truthfully say that in all that time, she has never intentionally hurt me. Through the years we have learned to trust each other on this point. This frees us from trying to read something sinister into one another's words or actions, and it serves as an effective cure for negative interpretations.

4. Avoidance and withdrawal

Some people find any discussion of a problem to be threatening, so they avoid it at all costs. They may change the subject or just not allow it to come up at all. The following conversation is an example of avoidance and withdrawal.

MARK: Whew! What a day! I'm so glad to be home.
KAREN: Hi, sweetie. I'm glad you're home too.
Mark gives Karen a quick hug, sits down, and picks up the remote.
KAREN: I've been waiting up for you. I've been waiting to talk to you.
MARK [*distracted*]: Hmm . . .

KAREN: You told Joey that he could build a ramp for his bike so he could learn to do tricks.

MARK: Honey, not now.

KAREN: If not now, when? It's always "not now" with you.

MARK: Soon. I've just got a lot on my plate right now.

KAREN: You always have a lot on your plate—every time there's something to be discussed. We've got to talk about this.

MARK: Why do you always want to fight? Can't you decide just to be happy?

KAREN: I don't want to fight. I want to talk. We need to settle this, to solve this together—as a team.

MARK: You may not want to fight, but these "discussions" always turn into one, and I just don't have the energy for it. Besides, Joey will be fine.

KAREN: This isn't about Joey. You don't ever want to discuss *anything*. How will we ever get things settled if we don't talk?

MARK: I can't talk right now. I've got to get to bed. I've got a big meeting tomorrow.

KAREN: Don't just walk out!

MARK: Good night!

It appears that Mark is using his long hours at work as a means of avoiding discussing problems with Karen. When he gets home, he's either too tired, too distracted, or it's just too late for serious talks, and he says he needs to get to sleep. As a result, issues are never resolved, and a wall of problems separates him from his wife.

Karen longs for the intimacy that resolved conflict brings. Her sincere desire is to work as a team with her husband. But Mark interprets Karen's efforts as simply attempts to pick a fight. Neither Mark nor Karen is getting what they want from their relationship. One feels attacked, and the other feels ignored and unimportant.

Mad About Negative Communication

I can't tell you how many times I've listened as someone has said sorrowfully, "My spouse and I never talk. We never deal with our problems. We just ignore them and hope they'll go away, but they never do."

To a person who wants to deal with an issue, avoidance of that issue feels like rejection. The spouse may be avoiding the issue to prevent the possibility of a fight, but to the person who wants to discuss the issue, it feels as though their spouse is avoiding them. It sends the message that they are so unimportant that their spouse doesn't even care to discuss problems with them.

Admittedly, many couples can't discuss a problem without allowing the discussion to deteriorate into a fight. They may need to see a counselor who can help them develop an effective way to solve the problem.

Eliminating negative communication patterns goes a long way toward communicating genuine care for one another. When couples remove negative patterns, they open themselves to receiving positive messages of love and concern without reservation. Since neither partner is intentionally sending mixed messages, they hear only their spouse's tenderness and love.

---

1. Howard Markman, Scott Stanley, and Susan L. Blumberg, *Fighting For Your Marriage: Positive Steps for Preventing Divorce and Preserving a Lasting Love* (Hoboken, N.J.: Jossey-Bass, 1994).

2. Ibid., 13–34.

Chapter 6
Mad About Forgiveness

We've dealt with a lot of very negative things in this book. By now you may be wondering if "madly in love" is even a possibility.

Truthfully, you can't be madly in love as long as infidelity, pornography, addiction, abuse, or negative communication exists in your marriage. Negative factors are so powerful that they make it almost impossible for people to appreciate anything positive that their spouse might add to their marriage; they'll view the positive as disingenuous. It does no good to send flowers to a woman who believes you don't respect her. Removing negative factors from your relationship does more to ensure the long-term survival of the marriage than does adding multiple positive factors. But here's the good news. Once the negative is gone, you and your spouse can appreciate the positives and the value and enjoyment they add to your marriage.

Forgiveness has elements of the negative—you need to forgive or be forgiven only when something hurtful has been done. And it's essential to removing that negative thing that caused the hurt from your marriage. But ultimately, forgiveness is a positive too. And so, in considering the positives, we'll begin with this one.

Fred's affair

Fred had been involved in an affair with someone at work. Lucy, his wife, was threatening divorce. The marriage was in real trouble. Just one thing prevented Lucy from ending it—she and Fred had three daughters who were crazy about their daddy.

Mad About Forgiveness

Fred confessed his infidelity and begged Lucy to forgive him, but Lucy was struggling. She didn't trust her husband. After all, if she forgave him, wouldn't that mean that what he had done really wasn't all that bad after all? And what would keep him from doing it again?

Lucy finally decided to do the work necessary to forgive her husband. Her heart softened, and she decided to become vulnerable to Fred once again. This was no easy task, and it required a great deal of effort from both Fred and Lucy, but eventually the work was done.

After Lucy forgave Fred, we began to work on other areas of their marriage, and things began to progress. However, they didn't progress nearly as quickly as they should have. Something was holding this couple back.

Eventually, we realized that although Lucy had forgiven her husband, Fred hadn't forgiven himself. He insisted on beating himself up for his transgression. His guilt and shame lowered his self-worth to the point that he was unable to accept Lucy's overtures of love, acceptance, and forgiveness.

When I pointed this out to Fred, he said he didn't deserve forgiveness. He also said he thought that if he forgave himself, he might be vulnerable to falling into an affair again.

It actually took more work for Fred to forgive himself than it did for Lucy to forgive him. Fred suffered greatly because of his transgression, but eventually he chose to forgive himself, and the marriage was saved. In fact, the marriage became stronger than it had been before the affair.

A few weeks after Fred finally forgave himself, another couple came to me for counseling. Julie and Tony were in real trouble. Julie had been unfaithful with someone at work. The affair had ended some months earlier, but Tony had just learned about it, and he was ready to end the marriage. Ten minutes into their story, I realized that Julie was the woman with whom Fred had his affair.

Mad About Marriage

Tony was reluctant to end his marriage to Julie because of what that might do to their two children. However, he had no desire to forgive her. We worked hard on this issue. I explained to the couple that unless Tony forgave Julie, there was no hope for the marriage. Tony understood this, but still he resisted.

Then, one evening, I asked Tony, "What is it that keeps you from forgiving your wife?"

After a long pause, Tony replied, "If I knew that the other man has suffered as much as I have, then I could forgive Julie."

I said, "You're telling me that you can't forgive your wife unless you know that the man with whom she had the affair has suffered as much as you?"

"Yes," Tony affirmed.

"Let me make sure I've got this straight," I said. "You're saying that if you could know with absolute certainty that the other man has experienced as much suffering as you have, then you would forgive Julie?"

"That's right. If I knew that to be the case, I could forgive her and move on," Tony said.

"Hold that thought," I said, and I left the room and went to the outer office. There I called Fred and asked for permission to share what he'd gone through as a result of his infidelity. When Fred gave his permission, I returned to my office, where Tony and Julie were sitting with puzzled looks on their faces.

"OK," I said. "Let me recap what you just said. You just told me that if you could know for certain that the other man had suffered as much as you, then you would forgive Julie. Is that correct?"

Hesitantly, Tony said, "Yeah, that's right."

I continued, "Well, I've got news for you. Ten minutes after you began telling me your story, I knew who you were. I knew the details of your story even before you shared them with me. I knew the story because I counseled the other couple, Fred and Lucy. They've given me permission to share their experience with you, and I can tell you without reservation that Fred has suffered even more than you have.

"Fred struggled to get his wife to forgive him, and then he agonized over forgiving himself. He's been wracked by guilt and shame for what he did to Lucy and their children, and even for what he's done to you. He went through a terrible depression, and he nearly lost his marriage—not only because of his infidelity but also because he was so angry with himself that he couldn't receive the love Lucy wanted to give him after she forgave him."

I paused to allow all that I'd said to sink in. You can't imagine the shocked looks that Tony and Julie had on their faces!

After a few moments I leaned forward and said, "Tony, now that you know this, what is it that keeps you from forgiving Julie?"

Tony's face was ashen, and he was absolutely speechless for a while. Finally, he answered me. "I guess nothing stands in my way," he said. And true to his word, Tony did the work necessary to forgive Julie. It wasn't easy, but he did it.

Forgiveness is an essential enzyme for every relationship. Without it, resentment builds and love dies. So, what keeps people from forgiving? I've heard people cite everything from "He doesn't deserve it" to "If I forgive her, she'll just do it again."

Does this sound familiar? Perhaps you have better reasons for not forgiving. But I ask, What happens if you fail to forgive?

Refusing to forgive doesn't hurt the offender nearly as badly as it hurts you. Carrying a grudge takes a tremendous amount of emotional energy. That energy could be better used for creative purposes. People who refuse to forgive rarely find genuine intimacy in their relationships. And unless both parties can find the strength to forgive the other, the marriage is in real trouble. If you ask me, these consequences amount to far too high a price to pay for what little satisfaction withholding forgiveness may give you.

What forgiveness means

What is forgiveness? It may actually be easier to say what it is not. Forgiveness is not forgetting. It may be impossible for you to forget. But the fact that you remember the wrong doesn't mean that you haven't forgiven it. (However, the fact that you remember it doesn't mean that you should bring it up in conversation with the person you have forgiven. More on that later!)

Forgiveness doesn't mean that your spouse's unfaithfulness didn't hurt or that it didn't matter. It doesn't mean that the wrong was actually right. It doesn't even mean that consequences for the action should be suspended. The person who committed the act may have to suffer consequences, but that doesn't mean you haven't forgiven them.

And grieving doesn't mean that you haven't forgiven someone. Some offenses result in a major loss. A woman can grieve the loss of the purity of her marriage even though she has forgiven her husband for an affair. Grieving is not the same thing as failing to forgive.

Forgiveness isn't a feeling. You may not feel that you have forgiven someone, and you may not feel that you have been forgiven, but it isn't wise to trust these emotions. It's better to trust the reality of forgiveness regardless of our feelings. If we depend upon our feelings, we may never experience the joy of forgiveness.

Forgiveness doesn't always mean reconciliation. In some cases, it isn't safe for you to be in a relationship with the person you need to forgive. This is especially true in cases of abuse, incest, or rape. You can forgive even the most horrific offenses, but that doesn't mean that you should put yourself back at risk with the person.

So what *is* forgiveness? It's a decision to put this offense in the past as you refuse to carry anger and resentment any longer. It's a forfeiture of your right to punish.

Please notice that I said forgiveness is a decision. It's a *decision* and not a *feeling*. If we *choose* to forgive in spite of our feelings, we can experience the relief that only forgiveness can bring. And when you decide to forgive someone and behave as though you have forgiven that person, eventually, in most cases, the feeling will follow. The same is true when you choose to believe in the reality of someone else's decision to forgive you and you behave as though you have been forgiven. Eventually, the feeling of having been forgiven will follow.

Without forgiveness, it is impossible for any relationship to last—to say nothing of its growing in genuine intimacy. No marriage can provide happiness or fulfillment if the past is constantly brought up and if resentment continues to increase.

Perhaps now you're convinced that you need to forgive your partner or even yourself, but you don't know how. I'm going to share a four-step process for forgiveness, but first let me say that what I am about to suggest is almost impossible for most humans to do. This process actually requires a miracle. The really good news is that when we move forward in faith, believing that the miracle of grace can occur in our lives, it can happen. We can experience forgiveness.

It's important to remember that even though forgiveness is a decision, it also requires a process. I may choose to forgive, but until I have done the work of forgiveness—until I have gone through the process of forgiving—my decision will be short lived.

For small hurts, completing this process may take only a few moments. For major issues, completing it can take weeks, months, or even years. Don't become anxious if the process doesn't produce forgiveness immediately. If you work the process regardless of how long it takes, you'll eventually arrive at the goal. Each step in the process requires a certain amount of work. If you try to hurry along to the next step without fulfilling the requirements of the previous one, you will thwart the process, and genuine forgiveness will elude you.

You may find it helpful—especially when you're dealing with big issues—to journal through each step. After you've completed the journal for a particular step, you may choose to read what you have written to someone you trust.

The four-step process

Step 1: Feel It. In this step we ask the questions "What happened to me?" and "How has it affected my life?" Be thorough with this step. You must know what you are forgiving before you can forgive. In this step you carefully outline the thing or things that were done to you and how those things have affected your life. You acknowledge that you were hurt and allow yourself to feel the pain that has resulted.

Melanie's grandfather molested her when she was a child. While Melanie didn't need to remember every incident of molestation, it was important that she list the type of things her grandfather perpetrated against her. Then it was necessary to explore how this had affected her physically, emotionally, mentally, and spiritually.

While Melanie's list is too long to share here, among the effects of the molestation was the fact that she began to view physical intimacy as the only way to be intimate with a man. She also saw herself as a "dirty" person. She viewed herself as someone who wasn't valuable in any way other than to provide physical pleasure for a man. Since she felt she deserved the treatment she received from her grandfather, Melanie also had a distorted view of God, believing that He disapproved of her.

Melanie had to list all of these effects of the molestation in order to know exactly what she needed to forgive. This was painful and laborious work. She was tempted to gloss over things, but her counselor's gentle persistence made certain she dealt with all the issues that arose as a result of the molestation.

When you've completed this step, you're ready to begin step number two.

Step 2: Own It. In this step we ask, "Who did this?" and "How do I feel about them?"

The first step dealt with the act itself and not with the person. Now we personalize it. Who did this? Name the person. Then write down how you feel about this person. Don't try to make this nice. Be honest about it.

We often have mixed feelings about people. In fact, we rarely feel 100 percent positive or 100 percent negative about anyone. We may feel real anger toward a person we truly love. For that reason, it may be helpful to say something such as "A part of me is very angry with this person." It may be equally true to say, "A part of me loves this person very much"! Combining those feelings into one statement may help put things into perspective. "A part of me wishes you would go away and never come back, but another part of me wants to reconcile with you and be together forever."

Some people feel that it is wrong or sinful to admit to feelings of anger, hatred, or rage. It isn't wrong for us to have those feelings. It's what we do with those feelings that matters.

Scripture helps us understand the proper way to deal with feelings that injury arouses. The psalms are particularly helpful in this regard. In Psalm 109, David prays about the enemies who had spread slanderous lies about him. The intensity of David's anger comes through clearly in this prayer.

May his days be few;
>   may another take his office!
May his children be fatherless
>   and his wife a widow!
May his children wander about and beg,
>   seeking food far from the ruins they inhabit!
May the creditor seize all that he has;
>   may strangers plunder the fruits of his toil!

Let there be none to extend kindness to him,
nor any to pity his fatherless children! (verses
8–12, ESV).

If you thought that it was sinful to express anger, these examples from Psalms should challenge your thinking. It isn't sinful to feel anger against those who wrong you, nor is it wrong to express that anger in appropriate ways. It *is* wrong to express those feelings and then never take the next step. The point is that expressing negative emotions in appropriate ways is a psychologically and spiritually healthy thing to do.

One appropriate way to share your negative feelings toward someone who has hurt you is through private prayer. Be honest and open about your emotions. Don't hold back. God already knows what you feel. You can't hide your feelings from Him. If you deny what you're really feeling, you only succeed in lying to yourself, and that lie will block your path to forgiveness and recovery.

Another appropriate way to express your feelings is to write them in a journal that you share with a counselor or trusted friend. This can be a very healing experience.

So, step 2 involves naming the perpetrator and identifying the emotions you feel toward that person.

Step 3: Fix It. If you stop with step 2, you will do nothing more than vent your rage. This doesn't fix the problem, and it won't take you to your ultimate goal, which is forgiveness. In the Fix It stage you ask, "Now that I know what happened, how it has affected my life, who did it, and how I feel about this person, what shall I do?" The answer is that you will choose to forgive this person.

It's important that you say, "I forgive you." The best way to do this may be through writing a letter of forgiveness. In some cases, rather than sending the letter to the offender, you should instead read it aloud to a person you trust—perhaps to a counselor. In the letter, state what it is this person has done that you are forgiving. You may need to state also the collateral damage you suffered as a result of the wrong done to you. For instance, Melanie could write, "Not only do I forgive you for molesting me as a child, but I forgive you for robbing me of a child's innocence and of the safety and security I should have experienced in your presence." She could include not only the molestation but also the collateral damage—the loss of innocence and of the sense of safety and security that a child should experience with her grandfather.

Remember that simply writing a letter and saying "I forgive you" may not change your feelings. We're dealing here with a decision to forgive. When you decide to forgive and you persist in that decision, the emotions are likely to follow eventually.

Remember also that deciding to forgive a person doesn't excuse that person or do away with the consequences of their behavior. It simply says, "I have decided that I won't carry the burden of anger and resentment that I have held against you. I have chosen to lay it down and to live free of its weight."

In cases where it would be impossible, unsafe, or inappropriate to share the letter with the offender, many people have found it helpful to do something else with it once they have written it. Some have shared the letter with a friend or counselor. Others have found it of value to use a tangible symbol of release, such as tying the letter to helium-filled balloons and sending it heavenward or burning the letter during a ceremony of their own creation. Such a ceremony may involve prayer, music, and the company of trusted friends.

A friend of mine found it helpful to decorate a box that she called her God Box. She said that whatever she placed in the box now belonged to God. She placed her forgiveness letter in the God Box to demonstrate that the issue now belonged to Him. Every time the offense comes to mind, she reminds herself that it no longer belongs to her; it belongs to God. And since it isn't her property, she has no right to it. This helps her avoid the temptation to hold on to the resentment.

Step 4: Leave It. During this step we ask, "How would I treat this person if they had never sinned against me?" In most cases, to treat the offender this way implies achieving reconciliation.

Before we go any further, allow me to offer this aside. In cases where it wouldn't be safe to establish an ongoing relationship with the offender, reconciliation is not only unnecessary, it's unwise. It may not be safe to reconcile with an abusive person or a child molester. Forgiveness doesn't always require reconciliation.

In most cases, however, reconciliation is a necessary final step to forgiveness. It may not happen overnight since rebuilding trust is a process. And the offender may have to prove himself or herself worthy of your trust. However, as day by day the offender demonstrates his or her worth, you will need to once again become open and vulnerable.

By the way, if reconciliation and restored intimacy are to occur, the offense must remain out of bounds for future arguments or disagreements. While it is true that you may always remember the offense, once you've forgiven it, you must never bring it up again. You must let it go and find a way to treat the offending party as though he or she had never sinned against you.

In most cases, as you persist in this new behavior—the behavior of forgiveness—you will find that feelings of forgiveness will follow. But even if those feelings don't come, forgiving someone means that you have left the past behind and won't revisit your formerly held anger and resentment.

Not only is it possible to forgive, it is also necessary to forgive. Don't give up. You can heal your marriage through the miracle of forgiveness.

Chapter 7
Mad About Sex

How would you like to postpone your death, improve your posture, boost your self-esteem, firm your tummy and hips, cut your risk of heart disease, reduce depression, and improve your overall fitness level? Research has discovered a wonderful natural treatment that won't cost you anything. And numerous studies have demonstrated that it will give you all of these benefits and more. What is it? Frequent lovemaking with your spouse!

You can make all kinds of jokes about this, but joking aside, there are lots of benefits to frequent sexual intimacy with your spouse. In addition to those I've already mentioned, here are a few more: marital sex makes you feel younger, reduces the risk of prostate cancer, offers pain relief, gives you a positive attitude, elevates your immune system, heightens sleep quality, improves your memory, increases your resistance to colds and flu, and—believe it or not—improves your sense of smell! Frequent sex also stimulates the growth of new dendrites in the brain, and studies have demonstrated that married couples who engage in frequent lovemaking feel more emotionally connected and that high-touch marriages are more satisfactory to the partners. All these research findings call for just one response: make love more often, right?

You might be tempted to agree; but I have to ask whether there's a direct cause-and-effect relationship between frequent physical intimacy and an improved marriage, or whether other factors are in play here too. Can we simply say, "If you want a better marriage, be sexually intimate more often"?

Frequent intimacy is probably a by-product rather than a cause of a healthy relationship. People whose marriages are plagued by the negative things we've discussed in this book are less likely to have the frequent, satisfying sexual intimacy that marriages that are relatively free of negative baggage benefit from.

What prevents couples from making love more often? The really big issues we've been discussing are the major hindrances. Abuse, addictions, infidelity, resentment, and negative communication kill frequent, high-quality sex. However, there are other, more minor factors that seem to get in the way too. Children tend to tire their parents, and they cut into their privacy and "together time," decreasing intimacy. Other factors include physical decline, frequent conflict, poor self-esteem, and a lack of spontaneity that dampens sexual passion and excitement.

Couples who want to improve their sex life need to pay attention to all of these factors. Determine which of them exist in your marriage, eliminate those that you can, and compensate for those you can't eliminate.

When you've eliminated the negative, it's time to add the positive. Act like you actually care about each other! Engage in conversation, gaze deeply into your partner's eyes, and learn the value of nonsexual touch. Schedule time for sex into your day, making it a high priority on your to-do list.

Successful couples learn that the nonsexual forms of intimacy pave the way to sexual intimacy. Eye contact is essential if couples want to have a sexual connection. Nonsexual hugging can lead to sexual hugging. Words of tenderness and appreciation can lead to physical expressions of love. Appreciation precedes affection, and affection precedes sexual intimacy.

By the way, the more you connect through touch, eye contact, conversation, and recreation, the less you'll be annoyed by petty little things. This form of nonsexual intimacy will reduce conflict in the marriage, and conflict is a major inhibitor of frequent sex.

Make intimacy a priority in your marriage. Both nonsexual and sexual intimacy will add value and pleasure to your marriage. Why wouldn't you do what it takes to fall madly in love?

Chapter 8
Mad About Spirituality

What, if anything, does spirituality have to do with your marriage? According to studies conducted between 1999 and 2003, quite a bit. Elizabeth E. George and Darren M. George cite these studies in their book *The Compatibility Code*.[1] They discovered that a husband's spirituality was positively associated with the level of marital satisfaction for both him and his wife. A wife's spirituality also has a positive impact, but at a lower level than that for husbands. In addition, when husbands and wives are members of the same church, their chances for marital fulfillment are significantly higher than those who are not. Denominational differences have a decidedly negative impact on the marriage.

In other words, if you want a better chance at having a successful and happy marriage, you should not only become a spiritual person, you should also marry a spiritual person from the same religious denomination as your own.

Another study links weekly church attendance with greater marital satisfaction. That study further states that when religion becomes personally relevant to a couple, they become happier with their marriage. By "personally relevant," I mean that religious values influence their decisions and behavior in everyday life. This includes things like frequent prayer and Bible study. The deeper the religious experience, the greater the marital satisfaction. And Larry Bumpass and James Sweet say that couples who attend church weekly are 35 percent less likely to divorce.[2]

Here's another statistic you'll like. A study titled *Faithful Attraction: Discovering Intimacy, Love, and Fidelity in American*

Marriage says that among couples who pray together regularly and have a high-quality sex life, only 1 percent think that divorce is a possibility for them![3] The most frequent description of the impact of spirituality on a marriage is that it strengthens the bond and makes couples feel closer.

What is spirituality? It is simply seeking the face of God. That means that while church attendance may assist people in their quest to find the face of God, spirituality is not equivalent to church attendance. Nor is it strict adherence to behavioral standards or understanding biblical prophecy and doctrine. In the right context, all of these things can be very good and can serve as aids to a person's search for the living God. But in and of themselves, they don't comprise spirituality. Many have attempted to substitute these things for spirituality, but every attempt to do so results in spiritual poverty and can actually be detrimental to marriage.

The quest for genuine spirituality begins with an acceptance of the gospel. And the gospel is the simple truth that salvation is offered to us as a gift because of the sacrifice Jesus made on the cross. When we accept the gospel, our sins are forgiven, and we are fully accepted by God. This means that we no longer have to live with guilt and shame. God loves us, accepts us, and forgives us.

Those who fail to recognize that the gospel a gift may attempt to earn God's favor through good behavior. This is a form of legalism and will always hurt one's marriage. Legalists develop judgmental attitudes and critical spirits. As they attempt to earn salvation, they begin to realize that they can never be good enough to obtain it. The only option, then, seems to be to compare themselves with others, and ultimately, to tear them down so in contrast they can look better.

Legalism offers no hope and no mercy. It results in controlling and destructive behaviors and attitudes. Being married to a legalist is a form of hell, because he or she will be critical of everything one says or does. No one, not even the legalist's spouse, will ever measure up to his or her standards, yet legalists are blind to their own imperfections.

The gospel declares that you are loved, accepted, and forgiven. When you realize that, you can love, accept, and forgive others. Is it any wonder that when spirituality begins with an acceptance of the gospel, the result is a marriage that makes one feel safe and secure?

The gospel makes a marked difference in a family, especially when the husband and father receives it. He sets the tone for the family, and as Elizabeth and Darren George's work informs us, the husband's spirituality has a powerful effect on the happiness and satisfaction found in the home. Positive, grace-filled spirituality connects us with the Source of love, life, joy, and abundant creation. As we connect to that Source, we are changed. Scripture tells us that we become like what we behold or admire. It follows, then, that when we admire the Source of love, we become more loving.

Spirituality fits us for relationships by contradicting pop culture's "me first" attitude. Jesus taught that the greatest commandments were love for God and love for our fellow human beings. That kind of love changes our attitude about life. It teaches us that every problem is a spiritual problem and thus requires a spiritual solution. When "love first" and "prayer first" replace "me first," one's marriage benefits.

Spiritual people have a foundation upon which to base their decisions. They realize the value of having a true North Star in life—a fixed point that never wavers and that tells them where they are in life and where they need to go to get to their destination, their goal. That North Star isn't just a set of rules; it's a relationship, and that relationship guides every facet of one's life.

Genuine spirituality also makes it possible for us to give and to receive forgiveness. Since Jesus has freely forgiven us, we are now free to forgive ourselves and others.

Why is it so hard?

If spirituality is so good for a marriage, why is it so hard to be spiritual?

To obtain genuine spirituality, we must surrender ourselves to Jesus—and, of course, in that act of surrender we lose control, or at least what we perceive as control. And like all human beings, we fear that loss of control.

Spirituality also requires vulnerability and openness. We tend to be private and protective about our spiritual life, but genuine spirituality places the intimate details of our hearts in open view. And we fear that if our spouse sees the ugly truth about who we are, he or she may lose respect for us or even reject us.

Many people have no model for what spirituality looks like in a marriage. If we didn't see this in our family of origin, we may not know how to practice it in our marriage. Adding another complication is the fact that husbands and wives may be at different spiritual levels. That can result in frustration or intimidation between marital partners.

How do we know whether we are experiencing authentic spiritual growth? I believe that there are only two appropriate measurements of spiritual life: Do I love God more today than I did yesterday? Do I love others more today than I did yesterday? If you can answer these questions in the affirmative, then you are growing spiritually.

There is a danger in all of this. That danger is seen in the difference between intrinsic spirituality and extrinsic spirituality.

Extrinsic spirituality has at its core a desire for personal gain. This type of spirituality is more concerned with social contacts or appearances than with commitment to God. In marriage, it tends to control rather than enable a spouse and family. Life decisions tend to be worse than those made by people who have an intrinsic spirituality, since they don't have the foundation of an authentic relationship with God.

Mad About Spirituality

Intrinsic spirituality grows out of deeply held beliefs. It involves a personal relationship with God in which one finds deep meaning. Intrinsic spirituality can't help but have an impact on one's attitudes and behaviors. It has a positive effect on marriage because it is genuine. Those whose spirituality is intrinsic make better life decisions because their decisions grow out of an authentic relationship with God and a positive commitment to Him.

Here are some ideas for making spirituality have the maximum impact on your marriage and family.

Share your walk. Share with those who are closest to you exactly how Jesus has influenced your life. Describe what your life was like before you met Jesus, and tell about the difference He's made for you. You've probably praised some product you've found helpful, so you shouldn't find it difficult to do the same regarding your walk with Christ.

Even though on the surface this may sound easy enough, many people find it very difficult to do. If that is the case for you, then perhaps you could start by sharing with your spouse something from a morning devotional, or you could choose a passage of Scripture for the day and share that passage.

If you aren't accustomed to talking about spiritual experiences and you feel intimidated by the thought of starting with your own mate or family, you might find it easier to join a small Bible study group and begin there. When you've mastered the art of sharing your experience with people you don't have to see every day, then you can carry your newfound skill home. While it requires a certain level of courage to begin sharing your spiritual journey, the potential benefits far outweigh the risks involved.

Share the impact of Scripture. Do you have a favorite Bible passage? If so, does your spouse know what that passage is and why it's so significant to you?

My favorite passage is Romans 10:9. I have a very personal

story about the impact that passage has had on my life. However, I didn't tell Gayle that story until years after we were married. All that time, my failure to share it with her served as a roadblock to a deeper level of intimacy and mutual understanding.

If Scripture hasn't been a part of your personal journey, you will find that your spiritual life will be greatly enhanced as you incorporate it into your everyday life. Start by reading and meditating on a few verses every day. Memorize Scripture using songs as an aid or by writing the passage out or repeating it aloud. As you do this, talk each day about what you've gained. Share your thoughts and insights on the passages. Tell how they have changed your attitudes and behaviors.

Studying the Bible together can be a great benefit to a marriage and to the larger family. When our children learned to read, we would give each of them a different version of Scripture and then take turns reading various passages aloud. We discussed the different wordings and talked about any insights the versions provided.

For generations, people have found the Bible to be a marvelous tool for the enhancement of the inner, spiritual life. It has served as an invaluable resource for bringing couples and families together. Don't ignore the means it provides to a deeper walk with Christ and a more meaningful and intimate marriage.

Pray together. Numerous pastors have told me that while they find it easy to pray in public, they are intimidated by the thought of praying with their spouse. Why would this be so difficult for someone whose profession involves a life of Bible study and prayer? Because prayer is the most intimate of spiritual activities. In prayer, we lay our souls bare before an all-knowing God—but while we may be able to trust Him with our innermost secrets, trusting our spouse is an entirely different story. Many fear that their spouse will think less of them when they discover an area of personal weakness or failure. Or, worse yet, that they might use this information against them.

A couple must have mutual trust before they can pray together with any degree of openness and vulnerability. If they don't have that level of trust, their marriage is in trouble.

So, for a couple to pray together, they must commit to being trustworthy and confidential. Being trustworthy means they will never use the information and insights gained through praying with their spouse against them or anyone else. Prayer is a private conversation between the two marriage partners and God. No one else should ever know what was said in that setting. When both parties are committed to trustworthiness and confidentiality, praying together can open depths of intimacy beyond description.

Busy schedules make it difficult to pray together, so intentionally look for opportunities to do so, or schedule prayer with your spouse into your day. Morning meals, evening meals, trips, and problems of various kinds provide excellent opportunities for spouses to have brief times of prayer together. I know of one man who calls his wife on her cell phone daily to pray with her.

Learn to pray together as a couple and as a family. It will make a difference in your marriage.

Worship together. It has been demonstrated that families who attend church together three or four times a month report far greater satisfaction with their marriage and are less likely to divorce than families who do not attend church together. Engaging in weekly worship attendance improves the quality of one's marriage.

In addition to weekly church attendance, it is important to engage in regular worship experiences as a couple and as a family. As I said above, I recommend reading and discussing Scripture as a couple, reading devotional materials together, or using audio or video devotional recordings. A variety of resources are also available that you can use to make family worships interesting.

Make worship a priority for your family. Weekly church attendance and regular private and family worship experiences will be of great value in your personal spiritual growth.

Take Communion together. Participating together in religious ceremonies that focus the attention on the saving grace of Christ strengthens the marital bond and promotes spiritual growth. As we partake of the bread and the wine—the emblems of Jesus' broken body and shed blood—we are reminded of the sacrifice made on our behalf. These symbols bring to mind the love, acceptance, and forgiveness we receive as gracious gifts from God through the atoning death of Jesus.

When we remember that God has forgiven and forgotten our sinful past, we are free not only to forgive ourselves, but also to forgive and accept our mate. Receiving the grace of God frees us to give that same grace to others. What better aid to marriage could there be?

Share a ministry together. Spirituality is not just about what we learn or experience for ourselves. Genuine spiritual growth requires service to others as well. When Gayle and I share a ministry of service to others, we find a higher level of intimacy with God and with each other.

Your church may have volunteer opportunities for you to choose from. These ministry opportunities may include volunteering at a homeless shelter, visiting people in hospitals or nursing homes, or a variety of other ministries to people in your community.

Gayle and I have served as leaders of children's or youth groups in our church. We have done everything from sponsoring outings and supervising them as they engage in community service to teaching their Bible lessons every week at church. We have loved the kids with whom we were so privileged to work, but we also fell more deeply in love with each other.

Mad About Spirituality

It is important that couples have shared goals, values, and purposes. Ministry to others provides a feeling of satisfaction as together we fulfill our purpose on earth. Giving back to the community can actually strengthen our relationship with God and with each other.

Sharing a ministry is a wonderful way to grow together in Christ. And growing together in Christ will have the added benefit of strengthening the marital bond.

---

1. Elizabeth E. George and Darren M. George, *The Compatibility Code: An Intelligent Woman's Guide to Dating and Marriage* (Garden City, N.Y.: Morgan James Publishing, 2009).

2. Larry L. Bumpass and James A. Sweet, "Cohabitation, Marriage, and Union Stability: Preliminary Findings from NSFH2" (NSFH working paper no. 65, Center for Demography and Ecology, University of Wisconsin, Madison, 1995).

3. A. M. Greeley, *Faithful Attraction: Discovering Intimacy, Love, and Fidelity in American Marriage* (New York: Thomas Doherty Associates, 1991); quoted in William R. Cashion and Joseph D. White, *7 Secrets of Successful Marriage* (2005).

Chapter 9
Flip the Switch

You can flip the switch from "just plain mad" to "madly in love." How? First, identity and remove the negative factors from your relationship. Forgive your spouse and yourself and be ready to move forward together.

Next, add the positive factors you need to make your marriage sweet. Settle for nothing less than an intimate marriage. Learn to identify and meet your partner's needs.

Above all, strive for genuine spirituality as you make God the Third Party in your marriage.

You can turn "just plain mad" into "madly in love." If you do, you'll find yourself positively "mad about marriage"!